MUSICAL INSTRUMENTS OF THE WORLD

Keyboards

Barrie Carson Turner
Illustrated by John See

Smart Apple Media

First published in the UK in 2000 by
Belitha Press Limited
London House, Great Eastern Wharf
Parkgate Road, London SW11 4NQ

Text by Barrie Carson Turner   Illustrations by John See
Text and illustrations copyright © Belitha Press Ltd 2000
Cover design by The Design Lab/Kathy Petelinsek

Published in the United States by
Smart Apple Media
1980 Lookout Drive
North Mankato, MN 56003

ISBN: 1-58340-062-1

Library of Congress Cataloging-in-Publication Data

Turner, Barrie Carson, 1951–
    Keyboards / Barry Carson Turner.
        p. cm — (Musical instruments of the world)
    Includes index.
    Summary: Describes eighteen keyboard instruments and how they are used,
including pianos, harpsichords, and synthesizers.
    ISBN 1-58340-062-1
    1. Keyboard instruments—Juvenile literature.
[1. Keyboard instruments.]   I. Title. II. Series.
ML549.T87   2000
786'.19—dc21   99-059873

Printed in Singapore

9 8 7 6 5 4 3 2 1

Picture acknowledgements: J. Allan Cash: 4-5, 14, 21; Eye
Ubiquitous: 23; Courtesy of Fenton House/National Trust: 7, 13, 15, 18,
27; The Lebrecht Collection: 22 Graham Salter/Courtesy of Finchcocks;
Redferns: 10 Odile Noel, 25 David Redfern; Mark Solomon: 19, 26;
Tony Stone Images: 11; John Walmsley: 6, 16.

Contents

Musical

Musical instruments are played in every country of the world. There are many thousands of different instruments of all shapes and sizes. They are often divided into four groups: strings, brass, percussion, and woodwind.

Percussion instruments are struck, shaken, or scraped to make their sound. Brass and woodwind instruments are blown to make their sound. String instruments sound when their strings vibrate.

instruments

This book is about keyboard instruments.
Keyboard instruments sound when their keys
are pressed. The keys on a piano operate small
hammers that strike the piano strings. The keys
on a church organ release air that is forced
through the organ pipes. An electronic keyboard,
or synthesizer, has keys that operate switches.
The switches make electronic sounds.

You can read about 18 different
keyboard instruments in this book.
There is a picture of each instrument
and a photograph of it being played.
On pages 30 and 31 you will find
a list of useful words to help you
understand more about music.

Upright piano

The upright piano takes its name from its shape. The strings are positioned vertically inside the wooden body. When the keys are pressed, small hammers strike the strings. There are two or three pedals at the bottom of the piano. They are worked by the player's feet to add variety to the sound of the instrument.

music stand

lid

The upright piano is designed to fit neatly against a wall.

keys

pedals

Fortepiano

Fortepiano is the name given to an early piano. The illustration shows the very first piano. It was invented and built by an Italian keyboard maker, Bartolomeo Cristofori, almost 300 years ago. The strings were struck by small, square hammers with leather tips.

lid

strings

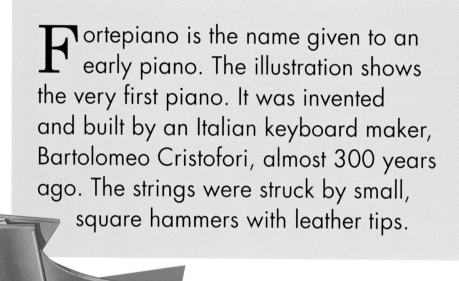

keyboard

The sound of the fortepiano is similar to the modern piano, but much less powerful.

Celesta

keys

The celesta (sel-es-ta) looks like a small piano. It was invented in 1886 by Auguste Mustel, a French instrument maker. Inside the wooden body are small steel plates. When the keys are pressed, tiny hammers hit the plates. This makes an attractive ringing sound.

The Russian composer Tchaikovsky wrote an important part for the celesta in the *Dance of the Sugar-Plum Fairy*. This piece of music appears in his ballet *Nutcracker*.

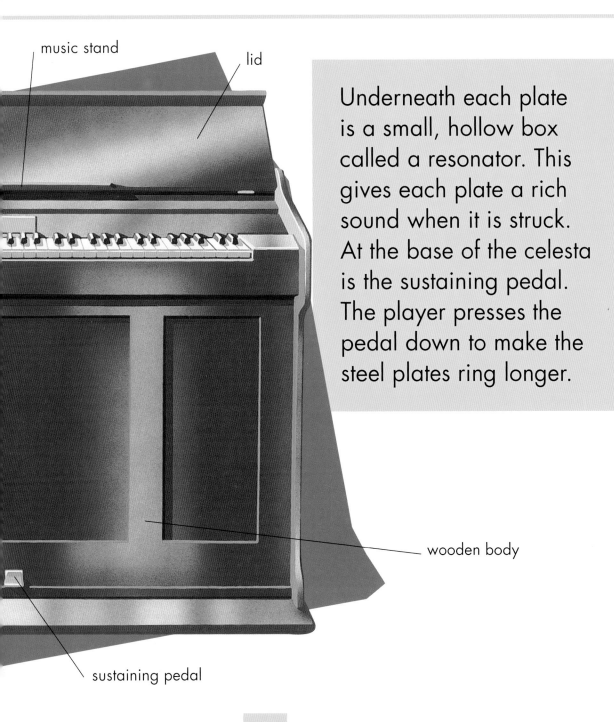

music stand

lid

wooden body

sustaining pedal

Underneath each plate is a small, hollow box called a resonator. This gives each plate a rich sound when it is struck. At the base of the celesta is the sustaining pedal. The player presses the pedal down to make the steel plates ring longer.

Melodica

The melodica makes a sound similar to the harmonica. Inside the plastic case are thin pieces of metal called reeds. When air is blown across the reeds, they vibrate, making the instrument sound. The player holds the melodica like a recorder and presses the keys to produce the notes.

plastic body

keys

blow hole

This unusual melodica has a miniature piano keyboard built into it.

10

Accordion

Inside the accordion are many thin reeds. Players squeeze the bellows in and out to force air across the reeds. This makes the accordion sound. The right hand plays the melody on the keyboard. The left hand presses in the finger buttons to produce the bass notes and chords.

bellows

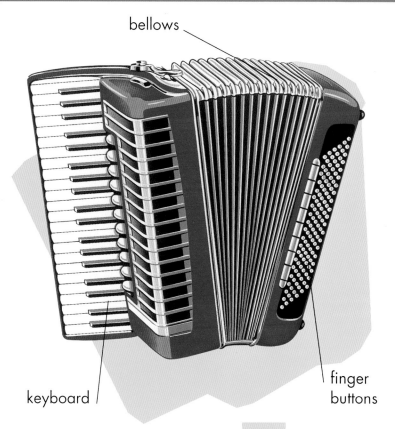

keyboard

finger buttons

The accordion hangs by shoulder straps, leaving both hands free to play.

Harpsichord

The harpsichord has been played since the 1400s. For 350 years it was the most common keyboard instrument. The harpsichord could make loud sounds, so it was ideal for playing in an orchestra. Today the harpsichord is used to perform only very old music.

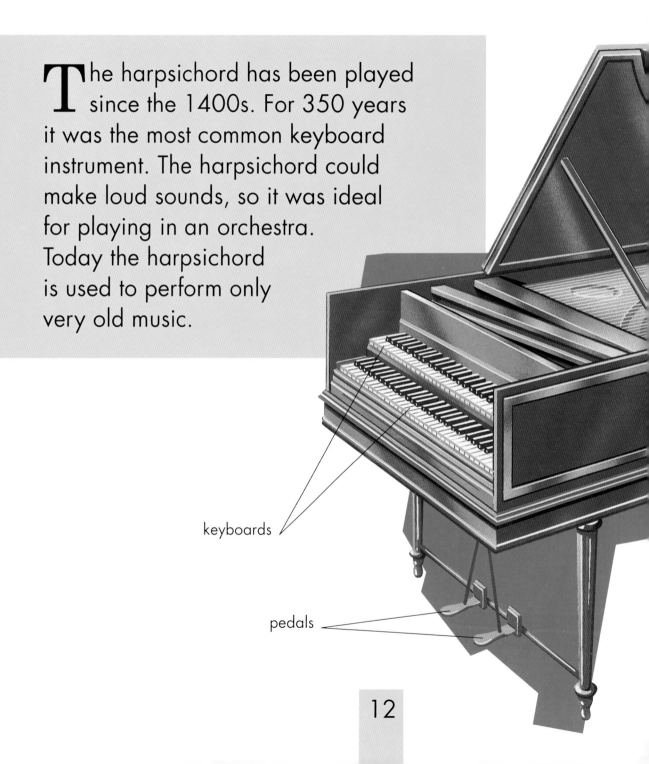

keyboards

pedals

lid

strings

When the keys are pressed, small quills pluck the strings. A quill is the hard spine of a bird's feather. There are two or more strings to each note. The player chooses how many strings are played by pulling out a small lever called a stop. Using all the strings makes the music loud. Using fewer strings makes the music softer.

Big harpsichords often have more than one keyboard. Each set of keys makes a different sound. This musician is playing on two keyboards at once.

Electronic organ

The electronic organ usually has at least two keyboards. These are called manuals. A row of pedals is played by the feet. The player presses switches, called stops, to make special sounds. Drum and percussion rhythms are programmed into the organ. They accompany the tune played by the organist.

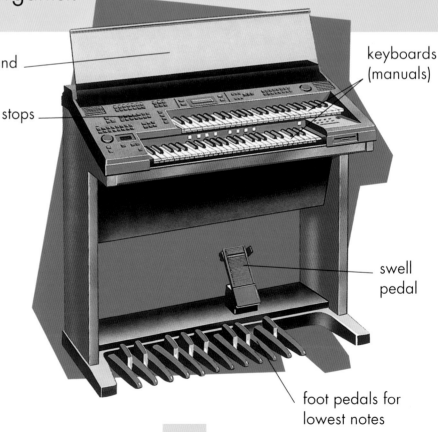

music stand

keyboards (manuals)

stops

Each manual on an organ has its own special sound.

swell pedal

foot pedals for lowest notes

Virginal

The virginal was first played almost 500 years ago. Some virginals are simple boxes that are played on a table. Others have their own legs. When the keys are pressed, small quills pluck the strings.

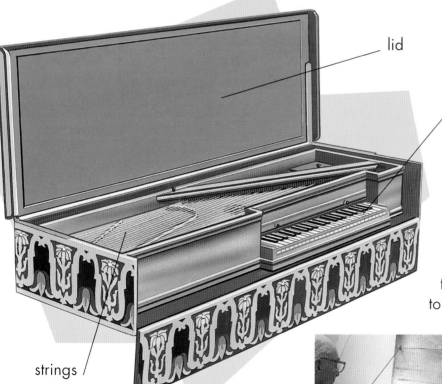

lid

keyboard

strings

The keyboard of the virginal is small, but the box must be large to hold the long strings.

Grand piano

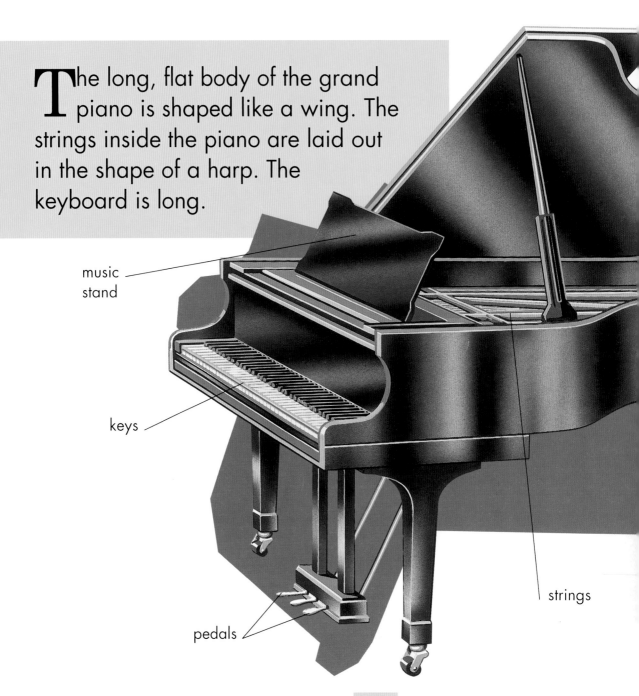

The long, flat body of the grand piano is shaped like a wing. The strings inside the piano are laid out in the shape of a harp. The keyboard is long.

music stand

keys

pedals

strings

The grand piano is too large for most houses. You will often see it at a concert. Here a grand piano is part of a school band.

lid

When the keys are pressed, small hammers strike the strings. The thick strings on the left side of the instrument make low sounds. The thin strings on the right make high sounds. Three pedals at the bottom of the piano control the sound of the instrument. They make the notes rich and strong or soft and gentle. When the piano is played in a large room, the lid can be opened to make the sound louder.

Clavichord

The clavichord, about 500 years old, was the first keyboard instrument that people played at home. It is shaped like a long box and is often played on a table. When the keys are pressed, small metal blades, called tangents, strike the strings. This is similar to the hammers striking the strings on a piano.

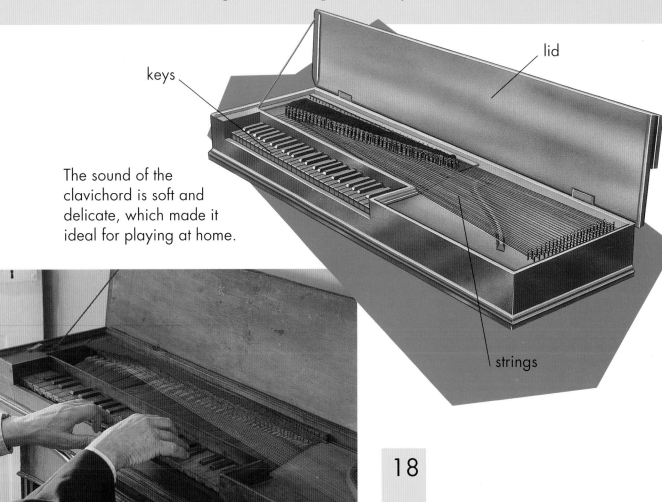

lid

keys

The sound of the clavichord is soft and delicate, which made it ideal for playing at home.

strings

Player piano

The player piano is automatic, so it needs no performer. Paper rolls punched with holes turn inside the piano. As the roll turns, the holes act like a code, telling the piano which notes to play. The illustration shows an early electric model. Other models are worked by bellows. The player piano can also be played like an ordinary piano. Another name for this instrument is pianola.

paper roll

electric light

music stand

keys

pedals

This player piano is worked by bellows. The musician presses them with his feet. The bellows blow air to turn the paper rolls.

Keyboards

Today the word "keyboards" is used to mean an electronic keyboard of any type. There are many different shapes and sizes of this instrument. Some of them are small enough to carry under your arm.

Keyboards have been used in rock, pop, and dance bands for more than 25 years. Several different keyboards may be played during a performance.

display screen

keys

control
buttons

Modern keyboards called synthesizers can copy the sounds made by many other instruments, including traditional keyboard instruments such as the piano and the organ. More unusual sounds played by a keyboard include ambulance sirens, ringing telephones, and even buzzing mosquitoes!

The electronic keyboard is one of the most exciting instruments to play. It can copy the sound of a complete orchestra.

Dulcitone

The first dulcitone (dul-si-tone) was made 200 years ago. Its original name was the tuning fork piano. Inside the wooden case is a row of metal bars. Each bar is shaped like the letter U. When the keys are pressed, small hammers strike the bars. Each bar sounds a different note.

lid

music stand

keys

pedal

wooden case

The sound made by the dulcitone is soft and mellow.

Hurdy-gurdy

The hurdy-gurdy rests on a player's lap or hangs by a neck strap. The strings are sounded by a wheel coated with a substance called rosin. The rosin helps the wheel to grip the strings and make a strong sound. When the keys are pressed, small wooden blades push against the strings to make the notes.

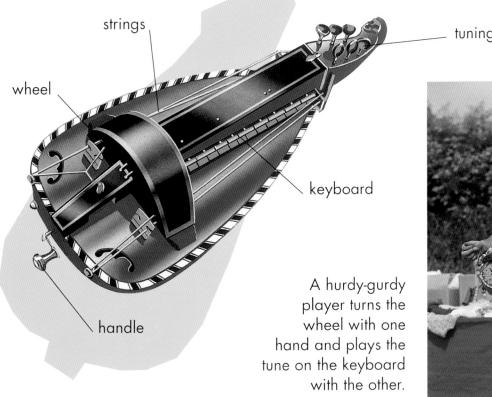

strings

tuning pegs

wheel

keyboard

handle

A hurdy-gurdy player turns the wheel with one hand and plays the tune on the keyboard with the other.

Church organ

The organ has been played for more than 2,000 years. It is the largest and loudest of all musical instruments. The first organs were pumped by hand. Modern organs have electric pumps. A church organ has several sets of pipes. On a large organ, some pipes are as long as 30 feet (10 m). Long pipes produce low notes. Short pipes produce high notes.

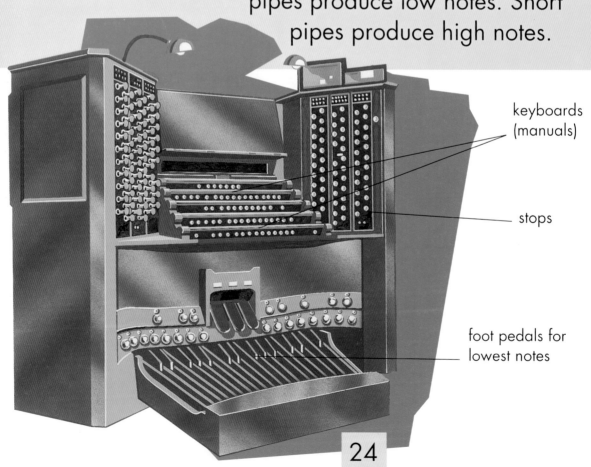

keyboards (manuals)

stops

foot pedals for lowest notes

pipes

When an organ is played, air is forced upward through a pipe. The air strikes the sharp edge of an opening cut into the metal. This makes the pipe sound. An organ usually has two or three keyboards. They are called manuals. Levers called stops are pushed in or pulled out to lead the air from one set of pipes to another.

The organist gives each manual its own sound by pulling out or pushing in the stops.

25

Digital piano

The digital piano has no strings. Each note is a recording taken from a real piano. When a key is pressed, the note sounds from a loudspeaker under the keyboard. The digital piano can copy the sounds of many other instruments. It can also record music played on it.

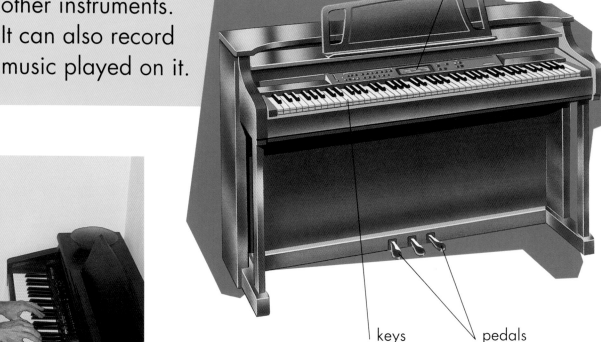

control panel

music stand

keys

pedals

The digital piano is played in exactly the same way as an ordinary piano.

Spinet

Before the invention of the piano, the spinet was one of the most popular home keyboard instruments. It works in the same way as its bigger cousin, the harpsichord. When the keys are pressed, tiny quills pluck the strings. This makes a quiet tinkling sound. A spinet cannot be played loudly.

strings

lid

keys

Spinets were often beautifully decorated, which made them popular as furniture.

Harmonium

The harmonium makes a sound similar to that of an organ. It contains many thin metal reeds. Because of this, another name given to the harmonium is reed organ.

At the base of the instrument are two bellows. Players press them in turn with their feet. The bellows pump air across the reeds, which vibrate to make the harmonium sound.

stops

keys

bellows

Above the keyboard is a row of levers called stops. Each stop may be pulled out or pushed in. This directs the air to different sets of reeds to produce a variety of sounds.

This small harmonium is from India. It is played sitting on the floor. The musician works the bellows with the left hand and plays the tune with the right hand.

Words to

accompany To play music with a singer or another player who carries the tune.

bass notes The lowest notes.

beat The steady pulse of the music.

bellows The part of an instrument that holds air. When a player squeezes the bellows, air is forced through the instrument to make sounds.

chords Groups of notes played together.

concert A performance by players or singers in front of an audience.

family (of instruments) Instruments that are similar to each other.

keyboard The row of keys on a keyboard instrument.

keys The small levers that a keyboard player presses to make the instrument sound.

manual An organ keyboard.

melody A tune.

musician Someone who plays an instrument or sings.

orchestra A large group of musicians playing together.

pedal Any part of an instrument worked by the player's foot.

percussion A family of instruments that are struck, shaken, or scraped to make their sound.

performer Someone who plays for or sings to other people.

pipe One of the metal or wooden tubes that make up an organ.

remember

quill The hard spine of a bird's feather.

reed A tiny, thin piece of metal or cane that vibrates when air is blown over it. Reeds make the sound in some keyboard instruments.

resonators Hollow boxes underneath the metal plates of a celesta. They make the sound of the instrument louder and fuller.

rhythm A rhythm is made by the beat of the music, and by how long and short the notes are.

rock A type of pop music that often has a strong beat.

rosin A substance that is rubbed onto the bows of string instruments and the wheel of a hurdy-gurdy to help grip the strings.

solo A piece played or sung by one player or singer.

stops Levers or knobs that change the sound of some keyboard instruments such as organs.

strike To hit the strings of an instrument.

sustaining pedal A lever operated by the foot that allows the notes of a keyboard instrument to sound for a longer period of time.

swell pedal A lever on an organ that increases the loudness of the instrument.

tangents Small metal blades that strike the strings of a clavichord.

vibrate The fast shaking of an object such as a string or a reed. Organ reeds vibrate when air is blown over them.

Index